Walking
in the
Power
of the
Holy Spirit

Paperback ISBN: 979-8-8229-4955-3

CHRISTOPHER SPENCER

Walking
in the
Power
of the
Holy Spirit

I'd like to dedicate this book to my mom because she has always been there for me, no matter what I was going through in my life. May God continue to bless her.

Contents

Introduction: Walking in the Power of the Holy Spirit — 1

The Reason Jesus Came to Earth — 3

Peter: The Perfect Example — 5

Your Flesh Did Not Get Saved — 7

Holy Spirit is My Navigator (GPS) — 8

It is Not About Us — 10

The Holy Spirit and His Power In the Beginning — 12

The Second Adam: Jesus Christ — 15

Love, Obedience, and Faith — 16

God's True Judgment: 1 Peter 2:23 — 19

To Truly Believe — 20

My Testimony — 22

About the Author — 24

Acknowledgements — 25

Introduction: Walking in the Power of the Holy Spirit

This is what all Christians need to have true success on this earth. In this book I will explain why it's God's purpose for us to have success and live an abundant life unto God.

In Genesis 1:1–2, it says, "In the beginning, God created the heavens and the earth. The earth was without form and void, and darkness was over the face of the deep. And the Spirit of God was hovering over the face of the waters." Genesis goes on to describe how God created the earth and man.

In Luke 10:18, Jesus said, "I saw Satan fall like lightning from heaven." So, we know Satan got kicked out of heaven. In Revelation 12:9, it says, "And the great dragon was thrown down that ancient serpent who is called the devil and Satan, the deceiver of the whole world—he was thrown down to the earth, and his angels were thrown down with him." It is key to remember that Satan is called a serpent. So, we know from Revelation that Satan was kicked out of heaven and kicked to earth. In Genesis 1:26–28, we read that God created man in His own image: "in the image of God he created him; male and female he created them" (Gen 1:27).

Now we know that Satan was kicked to earth, so I believe that since God kicked Satan and the angels who rebelled against Him out of heaven, that means they were already here when God created the earth and man. And Satan and his angels saw that God loved what He created. Satan knew God hated rebellion and sin, so Satan said, "If I can take what God hates and put it in what He loves, then that would cause a dilemma for God." So, in Genesis 3, we see that Satan deceived the woman (Eve) and she disobeyed God by eating the fruit from the tree of the knowledge of good and evil. Then she gave the fruit to Adam, which he bit into as well. And when they did this, sin came into man, for all mankind ever born would be in this fallen state of sin forever.

The Reason Jesus Came to Earth

Psalm 51:5 says, "Behold, I was brought forth in iniquity, and in sin did my mother conceive me." Now if one man's sin (disobedience) can leave all of mankind in a fallen state, then one man who knew no sin could come and die for all mankind. In 2 Corinthians 5:21, it says, "For our sake He made Him to be sin, who knew no sin, so that in Him we might become the righteousness of God."

So, Jesus came to earth and died on the cross for all those who believed in Him, giving us the opportunity to become new creatures in Christ.

Your flesh didn't get saved; when you believed in Jesus Christ and were born again, your flesh was not born again. Jesus said in John 3:5, "Truly, truly, I say to you, unless one is born of water and the spirit, he cannot enter the kingdom of God. That which is born of the flesh is flesh and that is born of the spirit is spirit."

Now when Jesus said born of water, He was talking about being baptized in water, and when He said born of the spirit, He was talking about being filled with the

Holy Spirit. Acts 1:5 says, "For John baptized with water, but you will be baptized with the Holy Spirit not many days from now."

Peter: The Perfect Example

While Jesus was on the earth, no one had more zeal for Christ than Peter. Peter was the only disciple bold enough to get out of the boat and walk on water (Matt 14:28–29). It was Peter who answered Jesus correctly when Jesus asked His disciples who He was (Matt 16:13–18). This same zealous Peter told Jesus that he would die for Him and would not deny Him (Matt 26:33–35). But Jesus told Peter that before the cock crowed that Peter would deny Him three times, and surely that is what Peter did (Matt 26:69–75). Peter had all that zeal for Christ, but when the time came for him to stand boldly for Christ, he failed. Yet this same Peter had one of the most awesome ministries for Christ after Christ's resurrection.

In Acts 3:1–11, Peter and John healed a crippled man at the gate called Beautiful. In Acts 5:15, it says, "So that they even carried out the sick into the streets and laid them on cots and mats, that as Peter came by at least his shadow might fall on some of them."

What changed in Peter's ministry? He denied Christ three times before the cock crowed, and yet he had a zeal for Christ when he was with Christ. The answer is in Acts 4:8 where it says, "Then Peter filled with the Holy Spirit said to them, 'Rulers of the people and elders.'" Peter—who denied Christ three times—stood before the rulers of the people and elders and declared Christ to them boldly.

When you allow the power of the Holy Spirit to lead and guide you, He will lead you into all truth.

Your Flesh Did Not Get Saved

When you were born again (which means believing in your heart and confessing with your mouth that Jesus died on the cross and was raised from the dead and now sits at the right hand of God the Father), the Spirit of God entered you, but your flesh was not born again.

Your flesh fights against the Spirit of God in you daily, so no matter what you do to please God, your flesh is there to war against the Spirit of God in you. Galatians 5:17 says, "For the desires of the flesh are against the spirit, and the desires the spirit are against the flesh, for these are opposed to each other, to keep you from doing the things you want to do."

This is why we must get the word of God in us so we can bring our flesh under subjection to the Spirit of God, and this is why Jesus came to earth to show us how to walk in the Spirit while in the flesh. When He died on the cross and rose again, He took victory from the grave and the sting out of death for those who believe in Him.

Holy Spirit is My Navigator (GPS)

When Jesus rose from the dead and went back to God, His Father, He sent the Holy Spirt to dwell in us and lead and guide us into all truth. John 16:7 says, "Nevertheless, I tell you the truth: it is to your advantage that I go away for if I do not go away, the Helper (Holy Spirit) will not come for you. But if I go, I will send Him to you." John 16:13 says, "When the Spirit of truth comes, he will guide you into all the truth, for he will not speak on his own authority, but whatever he hears, he will speak, and he will declare to you the things that are to come." The Holy Spirit is our last chance to believe God through Jesus Christ, and that is why Jesus said in Matthew 12:31–32, "Therefore I tell you, every sin and blasphemy will be forgiven people, but the blasphemy against the Holy Spirit will not be forgiven. And whoever speaks against the Son of Man will be forgiven, but whoever speaks gains the Holy Spirit will not be forgiven, either in this age or in the age to come."

The Holy Spirit is the key to living an eternal life with Christ Jesus and God. The Holy Spirit and His power in us manifests healing in our bodies that drives out demons that enables us to speak what God wants us to say on this earth so His glory will be manifested in this earth.

It is Not About Us

When Jesus was on the earth, He taught us that it was not about Him and that everything He did was because God, His Father, showed and told Him to do it. He took no credit on His own, and He was always glorifying His Father. In Mark 10:18 and Luke 18:19, Jesus says, "Why do you call me good? No one is good except God alone."

We must know that we are but vessels for God to be used on this earth through Jesus Christ by the Holy Spirit and His power. Jesus also said in John 5:19, "Truly, truly I say to you, the Son can do nothing of His own accord, but only what He sees the Father doing. For whatever the Father does, that the Son does likewise."

Without the Holy Spirit, you cannot be a part of God's kingdom, because when you die your flesh returns back to the ground from where it came, and your spirit returns back to God who gave it (Eccl 12:7).

In conclusion, the Holy Spirit is our last and only hope of having an eternal life with God through Jesus

Christ. Therefore, we must yield daily to the Holy Spirit and His power that we may be true vessels of God on this earth, walking in the power of God as Jesus showed His disciples and as they in turn showed us.

In John 14:15–16, Jesus says to His disciples, "If you love me, you will keep my commandments. And I will ask the Father, and He will give you another Helper to be with you forever."

The Holy Spirit and His Power In the Beginning

In Genesis 1:2, the Bible says, "The earth was without form," (meaning it lacked order and content) "and void, and darkness was over the face of the deep and the Spirit of God was hovering over the face of the waters." So, the earth was dark, (Gen 3) without shape, and mostly water, if not all water (Gen 6).

Now we know the serpent, which is called the devil or Satan (Rev 12:9), is related, because in Luke 10:18, Jesus said, "I saw Satan fall like lightning from heaven. Behold, I have given you authority to tread on serpents and scorpions and over all the power of the enemy and nothing shall hurt you."

I believe that when God created the earth that Satan was already here on earth, because Jesus said "I saw Satan fall from heaven like lightning." So, God kicked Satan out of heaven along with one-third of the angels (Rev 12:4). In other words, God said, "I whooped your tail in heaven (which is God's throne), and now I am coming to earth where I kicked you and one-third of the angels, which took your side when you rebelled against me, and I am going to create on earth and whoop your tail down here too." So, Satan was already here on earth (Rev 12:12).

I believe that Satan watched as God formed and populated the earth and when he saw that God loved what He created (Gen 1:31), he said, "If I can take what he hates, which is sin, and put it in what he loves, which is man (John 3:16), that will put God in a dilemma." When God said "let us make man in our image" (Gen 1:26), I believe He was talking to Jesus and the Holy Spirit (John 17:5).

Now when Adam and Eve sinned (Gen 3:6), they cursed all men (Rom 5:12). So, God had a plan to redeem man. If one man (Adam) could cause all to sin or be cursed, then one man (Jesus) could take away all sin and removed the curse (Rom 5:17).

So, now that Satan and his angels are on the earth, they need a body to do their evil, just as the Spirit of God needed a body to fulfill God's plan of reconciling man back to Him through Jesus Christ (2 Cor 5:19). So, unless you believe (give your life to Christ), you are an excellent target for Satan to use you against the plan of God.

But we know that Satan and all those he has deceived will be defeated (Rev 20:10). Because Adam was the first man, he represented all who would descend from him. From the very beginning, God put the plan in motion to send his Son. Jesus Christ, to redeem and reconcile man back to Himself (2 Cor 5:19).

Because of Adam, we were born spiritually dead, so Jesus Christ came to die for our sins so that we could be in right standing with God. But redemption is ours only if we believe that Christ died for our sins and live our lives through Christ guided by the Holy Spirit.

Death is never natural, but is the last enemy that will be conquered finally and forever at the return of Christ. The grace of God given to followers of Christ triumphs over sin and death (Rom 6:14).

So now that we live our lives through Christ, sin has no more power over us. But does that mean we never sin again? No! It means that the normal pattern of life for Christians should be progressive growth in sanctification, resulting in ever greater maturity and conformity to God's moral law in thought and action. Knowing that the flesh is warring against the Spirit of God, we should continue to stay in God's word so we can bring our flesh under subjection to the Spirit of God. For Romans 8:7–8, says, "For the mind that is set on the flesh is hostile to God, for it does not submit to God's law; indeed it cannot. Those who are in the flesh cannot please God."

The Second Adam: Jesus Christ

God created Adam for the purpose of being His agent or representative on earth, so He gave man dominion and authority over the earth, but with that dominion and authority came instructions. When Adam and Eve disobeyed and rebelled against God because the serpent deceived them, Adam and Eve died spiritually as God had told them in Genesis 2:17. Though they lived many more years, it was outside of what God had intended for them.

So, Christ Jesus had to come to earth and fix what Adam messed up. Just as one man caused all to sin, one perfect man who knew no sin could come and die for all who have and will sin. In other words, He took our place and gave us a chance to be redeemed back to God. But this is only possible if we allow the Holy Spirit to teach and guide us as we live a life through Christ Jesus.

Love, Obedience, and Faith

Love, obedience, and faith are the three keys to living a successful and pleasing life unto God.

God is love, and love is one of the fruits of the Holy Spirit (Gal 5:22–23). Obedience is the act that shows we love God (John 14:15). We aim to keep all His commandments (not just the ten). Faith is believing and trusting God that He will do what His word said He would do, no matter the circumstance, trial, or tribulation. We must know that this walk of faith following Jesus is not easy, and the Bible never said it would be easy, but God's word says, "My brethren, count it all joy when you fall into various trials, knowing that the testing of your faith produces patience. But let patience have its perfect work, that you may be perfect and complete, lacking nothing" (Jas 1:2–4).

A few words of wisdom: a building doesn't make a church, but true believers do. We are to long for God's word so that we will continue to grow in faith. We are like living stones which together build a spiritual house with Christ Jesus as the cornerstone. Holding on to sinful desires brings spiritual harm.

Worry is a form of pride because it involves taking concerns upon oneself instead of entrusting them to God. Believers can trust God because, as our Father, He cares for us. 1 Peter 5:6–7 says, "Humble yourselves, therefore, under God's mighty hand, that he may lift you up in due time. Cast all your cares on him because he cares for you."

A fleshly minded Christian desires the things of the flesh. Galatians 5:19–21 says, "Now the acts of the sinful nature are obvious: sexual immorality, impurity, sensuality, idolatry, sorcery, enmity, strife, jealousy, fits of anger, rivalries, dissensions, divisions, envy, drunkenness, orgies and things like these. I warned you, as I warned you before that those who do such things will not inherit the kingdom of God."

A spiritually minded Christian desires the things of the spirit, such as studying the word of God, praying, fasting, and allowing the Holy Spirit to guide and teach you. Galatians 5:22–24 says, "But the fruit of the Spirit is love, joy, peace, patience, kindness, goodness, faithfulness, gentleness, self-control; against such things there is no law. And those who belong to Christ Jesus have crucified the flesh with its passions and desires."

Every time you are tempted when you are weak and you pass the test, you are strengthened in that area where you were weak. Don't be blinded by fleshly desires. Fleshly desires are things such as power over people: lust (desires) of the flesh, fame, greed, or anything that feeds the flesh. Because when you are blinded by fleshly desires, you cannot see spiritually.

Matthew 27:1 says, "When morning came, all the chief priests and elders of the people took counsel against Jesus to put Him to death." Now these were people in the church trying to kill the one who is the head of the Church.

God's True Judgment: 1 Peter 2:23

When Christ suffered, He did not threaten. It is common to long for retaliation in the face of unjust criticism or suffering, but Jesus behaved like a meek lamb (Isa 53:7). He could do so because He continued entrusting both Himself and those who mistreated Him entirely to God, knowing that God is just and will make all things right in the end. Likewise, as believers, knowing God is a just God and judges justly, we are able to forgive others and to entrust all judgment and vengeance to God. We know every wrong deed in the universe will either be covered by the blood of Christ or be repaid justly by God at the final judgment, but we can't do this without the Holy Spirit leading us. This means we must bring our flesh under the power of the Holy Spirit by saying to the Holy Spirit, "I surrender—have your way."

To Truly Believe

When we are born again, we believe that Jesus Christ died for our sins and is now at the right hand of God our Father.

To believe in the Lord Jesus Christ means more than intellectually acknowledging Him or believing certain facts and truths about Him. Our faith must be active. drawing other people to recognize and accept Jesus as both Savior and Lord, the forgiver of their sins and leader of their lives.

Saving faith accepts what Jesus Christ has done to provide forgiveness for one's offenses against God and then surrenders and entrusts the leadership of one's life to Christ. When a person demonstrates this kind of faith in Christ, he or she becomes a child of God, enters into a personal relationship with Jesus Christ, and receives the Holy Spirit as a constant help, guide, and comfort. The Holy Spirit will continually draw the person's attention to Jesus Christ and bring him or her into a closer relationship with Jesus Christ.

The reason why we must keep running after God *first*, even when we are temped and sin in the flesh, is because in 2 Peter 2:9, the Bible says, "The Lord knoweth how to deliver the godly, out of temptation and reserve the unjust unto the day of judgement to be punished." What makes you godly is that you keep God *first* in your life. Proverbs 24:16 says, "For the righteous falls seven times and rises again, but the wicked stumble in times of calamity." What makes that righteous man get up every time? It is his faith in the word of God. So, whatever you do, please do not lose your faith in God and His word.

In Luke 22:32, Jesus told Peter, "But I have prayed for you that your faith may not fail. And when you have turned again, strengthen your brothers."

My Testimony

In the early '90s, I got addicted to crack cocaine, and my life was a living hell for two years. I worked, but I did not pay my bills because I used my money to purchase crack. I got tired of struggling, so I tried to get off crack on my own, but I was not strong enough. I prayed to God to deliver me from crack, and He started the process. But I still had a yearning and craving for it. I kept going back to using crack. But it was never the same after I prayed to God. Each time I used crack, a fear of judgment came over me. I was fearful that something bad was going to happen to me because I was taking the advantage of the grace of God. Hebrews 10:26–27 says, "For if we go on sinning deliberately after receiving the knowledge of the truth, there no longer remains a sacrifice for sins, but a fearful expectation of judgement and a fury of fire that will consume the adversaries."

A few months later, I was still pleading with God while using crack saying, "Father, you said ask anything like You and You will do it! I am going to keep coming to You until you do it." I could hear the enemy saying it had been all these months and it had not happened yet, so I said, "Lord, I am going coming after you or die trying to get to you."

But it was only when I said "Holy Spirit, I surrender" that the Holy Spirit came over me. and just like that the addiction to crack was over. I became a new person. The person who was on crack was dead. I did not talk the same way or think the same way or do the same things. In 2 Corinthians 5:17 it says, "Therefore, if anyone is in Christ, he is a new creation. The old has passed away, behold the new has come." It was like I had to get on crack to get to know the manifested power of the Holy Spirit, but that is not true, it just seemed that way. In Romans 8:28 it says, "And we know that for those who love God all things work together for good for those who are called according to His purpose." It has been over thirty years since I last did crack cocaine, and not once have I desired to do it again. That is what seeking God and surrendering to the Holy Spirit will do for you.

About the Author

Chris Spencer loves the Lord and has been a born-again believer since 1995. His desire is to be true vessel for God to use to advance the Kingdom of God and to tell others that Jesus Christ left us with the Holy Spirit and His power to live in us so we can live a life pleasing and acceptable to God as Jesus showed us while He was on the earth.

Acknowledgements

I'd like to acknowledge some of the ministries and pastors that have sowed into my life and my continuing walk with God. May God continue to bless these ministries and there leaders and there the families

The Potters House - Bishop T.D Jakes

Upper Room - Bishop Patrick L. Wooden

Word of God fellowship - Bishop Frank & Pastor JoeNelle Summerfield

Cross Assembly(Raleigh, N.C.) - Pastor Chad Harvey